21st CENTURY LIVES
CELEBRITY CHEFS

Debbie Foy

WAYLAND

First published in 2010 by Wayland

Copyright © Wayland 2010

Wayland
338 Euston Road
London NW1 3BH

Wayland Australia
Level 17/207 Kent Street
Sydney, NSW 2000

Senior editor: Camilla Lloyd
Designer: Steven Prosser
Picture researcher: Shelley Noronha

Picture Acknowledgments: The author and publisher would like to thank the following for allowing their pictures to be reproduced in this publication: Cover & 16: © Rex Features; © Danny Martindale/Getty Images: 1 & 10; © Rex Features: 4, 7, 21; © Katie Collins/Getty Images: 5; © Danny Martindale/Getty Images Linder: 6; © Lisa Linder: 8; © BBC/Todd Antony: 9; © Mark Whitefield/Rex Features: 11; © David Hartley/Rex Features: 12; © Andy Weekes/Rex Features: 13; © Rune Hellestad/Corbis: 14; © Justin Lloyd/Newspix/Rex Features: 15; © Eddie Mulholland/Rex Features: 17; © Myung Jung Kim/Press Association Images: 18; © Rui Vieira/Press Association Images: 19; © Geoffrey Swaine/Rex Features: 20.

British Library Cataloguing in Publication Data:
Foy, Debbie.
   Celebrity chefs. -- (21st century lives)
   1. Cooks--Biography--Juvenile literature.
   I. Title II. Series
   641.5'0922-dc22

ISBN: 978 0 7502 6205 7

Printed in China

Wayland is a division of Hachette Children's Books, an Hachette UK company.

www.hachette.co.uk

Contents

Some definitions:
Awards in this book were given for services to the food industry.
CBE – Commander of the Order of the British Empire.
MBE – Member of the Order of the British Empire.
OBE – Officer of the Order of the British Empire.

Delia Smith
The original TV chef

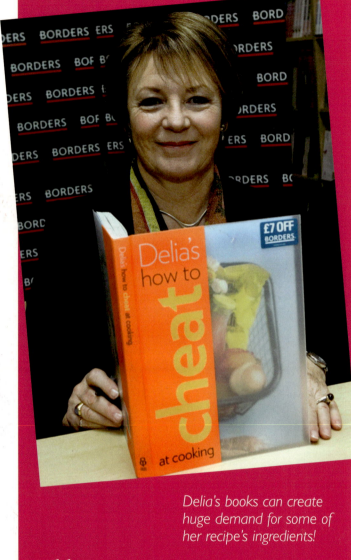

Delia's books can create huge demand for some of her recipe's ingredients!

> **"I think I will have performed a great service if I can make it possible for families to sit round and eat a meal together. That's my mission."**

Delia Smith to the *Guardian*, 2008

Name: Delia Smith CBE

Date and place of birth: 18 June 1941 in Woking, Surrey

Background: Delia attended Bexleyheath School, leaving at 16 with no qualifications. She worked as a hairdresser, in a travel agents and as a shop assistant. At 21 she started working at a restaurant in London called The Singing Chef, doing the washing up and waiting tables before becoming a cook.

How she started cooking: While working at the restaurant, Delia became interested in the history of English cooking. She used to visit the Reading Room at the British Museum to study 18th Century cookbooks, copying down the recipes and trying them at home. She began writing a cookery column for the *Daily Mirror*, and published her first book *How To Cheat At Cooking* in 1971.

Big break: Delia's TV career began in 1973 with a series called *Family Fare*, but it was *Delia Smith's Cookery Course* (1978–81) that made her a household name. She also regularly appeared on BBC's Saturday morning children's TV alongside Noel Edmonds, doing basic cooking demonstrations.

Popular TV shows: *Delia Smith's Christmas* (1990), *Delia Smith's Summer Collection* (1993), *Delia Smith's Winter Collection* (1995-96), *Delia's How To Cook* (1998-2002), *Delia* (2008), *Delia Through The Decades* (2010).

Major achievements: She is the UK's best selling cookery author, and has sold more than 19 million copies of her books.

Something you might not know about her: Delia baked the cake that appears on the cover of the Rolling Stones album *Let It Bleed* (1969).

In 2010, Delia and Heston Blumenthal became the faces of Waitrose supermarket. They are a great combination because Delia knows how to knock up tasty meals and Heston is very inventive with his ingredients.

Delia Smith is Britain's favourite cookery writer. Her first book was published in 1971, and her most recent and revised, *Delia's How To Cheat At Cooking* (2008) sold faster than Katie Price's autobiography, and the latest books from Jamie Oliver and Nigella Lawson put together.

Amazingly for someone who doesn't know how to use a computer, Delia has been writing about food for over 40 years. In 1969 she became cookery editor for the *Daily Mirror*, where she met her future husband Michael Wynn-Jones. In 1972 she started writing a column for the *Evening Standard* newspaper in London, which she wrote for 12 years. She also wrote a column for the *Radio Times* until 1986.

It was Delia's no-frills approach to TV presenting that really made her famous. Throughout the 1970s, 1980s and 1990s she seemed to be ever-present on our screens. She hosted a number of very popular series under her own name, and was also a regular guest on Saturday morning children's TV, demonstrating simple recipes that viewers could try at home. Her most recent series, *Delia Through The Decades*, a look back at her 40-year career, was broadcast in early 2010.

Delia has been a season ticket holder at Norwich City football club since the 1970s. She and her husband have been majority shareholders at the club since 1996, when they invested £1 million to join the board. Not surprisingly, the club now has six excellent restaurants that turn over nearly £4 million per year.

Her books are known to have 'the Delia effect' – producing steep sales increases on products she has included in her recipes. *Delia's How To Cook* (1998) led to a 10 per cent rise in egg sales, and her latest book *Delia's How To Cheat At Cooking* (2008) boosted sales of Marks & Spencer minced lamb by 200 per cent and Asda frozen chargrilled aubergine slices by 150 per cent. Delia's formula is based on presenting real food to real people and it has made her a huge success.

"Delia [made] the food the star. She was talking to you, not as a teacher, but as a friend. That was the atmosphere she created from day one."

Deborah Owen in the *Telegraph*, 2008

Gordon Ramsay
The world's most famous chef

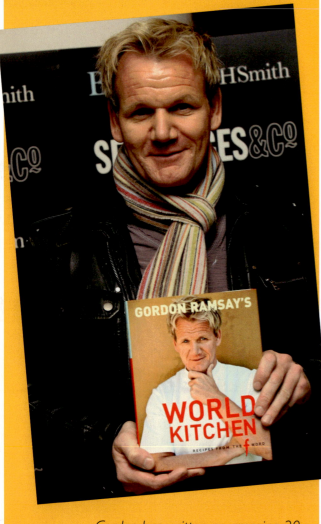

Gordon has written an amazing 20 cookbooks in the last 15 years!

"**I cook, I create, I'm incredibly excited by what I do. I've still got a lot to achieve... If I relaxed, if I took my foot off the gas I would probably die.**"

Gordon Ramsay to the *Telegraph*, 2009

Name: Gordon James Ramsay Junior OBE

Date and place of birth: 8 November 1966 in Elderslie, Renfrewshire, Scotland; he grew up in Stratford-upon-Avon

Background: Gordon was forced to give up a promising football career because of an injury. He wanted to join the navy or the police, but lacked the necessary qualifications so he enrolled at a local college to study hotel management.

How he started cooking: In the late 1980s, Gordon was working at local hotels and restaurants. He moved to London and found a job with Marco Pierre White at Harvey's. From there, he worked for Albert Roux at Le Gavroche in Mayfair, then moved to Paris for three years to work for Michelin-starred chefs Guy Savoy and Joel Robuchon. The Michelin Guide is a series of annual guide books that awards one to three stars to restaurants of outstanding quality. There are less than one hundred three-star restaurants in the world.

Big break: Returning to London in 1993, Gordon was offered the position of head chef at Marco Pierre White's Aubergine, and quickly won two Michelin stars. He opened his own restaurant in 1998, and has continued to expand ever since. Gordon now owns restaurants in New York, Tokyo and Los Angeles among other cities.

Popular TV shows: Gordon's first TV shows were the documentaries *Boiling Point* (1998) and *Beyond Boiling Point* (2000), which followed his attempts to gain three Michelin stars. Since then he has fronted *Ramsay's Kitchen Nightmares* (from 2004), *The F-Word* (from 2005), *Hell's Kitchen* (from 2004) and *Hell's Kitchen USA* (from 2005).

Major achievements: Gordon has been awarded 12 Michelin stars during his career, and is one of only three UK chefs to maintain three stars at the same time.

Something you might not know about him: Gordon was voted most terrifying celebrity in a *Radio Times* poll.

A fiery temper and a desire for perfection always make Gordon's TV appearances highly entertaining.

Four years later he had won two Michelin stars at Marco Pierre White's Aubergine, before leaving to set up the first of his own restaurants, Gordon Ramsay at Royal Hospital Road. Gordon's restaurant business has since grown to include Petrus in London (where six bankers famously spent £44,000 on wine during a single meal!), Amaryllis in Glasgow, Gordon Ramsay at Claridge's, Verre in Dubai, Gordon Ramsay at the London in New York City, and many others.

However, Gordon is just as well known for his TV shows. *Ramsay's Kitchen Nightmares* (Channel 4) sees him visit struggling restaurants and help sort out their problems. The show first aired in 2004 and is still running today, with an American version that launched in 2007. *The F-Word* (a reference to Ramsay's regular swearing) was launched in 2005 – also on Channel 4 – and is part chat show, part food documentary and part travel show. In the most recent series, Gordon organised a competition to find the UK's best local restaurant. Gordon married Tana Hutcheson in 1996, and they have four children. Since 1996 he has also written 20 books, and contributes a weekly food and drink column to *The Times*' Saturday magazine. When does he find time to sleep?

Gordon Ramsay is famous for his quick temper, loud mouth, and plain-speaking style. He's the chef who went from chopping vegetables in pub kitchens to running a multimillion pound restaurant empire, and fronting TV shows on both sides of the Atlantic. He is a fantastic, inspired cook who has won 12 Michelin stars, and managed some of the most famous restaurants in the country.

Gordon's childhood was tough. His family travelled constantly, and he left school with only a handful of formal qualifications. He enrolled in a hotel management course 'by accident' and soon found himself working for some of the best – and most demanding – chefs in the world. He worked alongside Marco Pierre White and Albert Roux in London, and then Guy Savoy and Joel Robuchon in Paris. After a year working as a personal chef on a private yacht, Gordon returned to London determined to make his own mark on the restaurant business.

"Argumentative, brash and confrontational, Gordon Ramsay is as well known for his bad temper... as for his unquestionable culinary flair."

Jonathan Thompson in *The Times*, 2007

Anjum Anand
TV's tastiest cook

Anjum left a career in international business to become a TV chef and cookery writer.

> **"My mission in life is to take the fear out of Indian food. I want to show that it can be healthy, nutritious, light and easy to throw together."**
>
> **Anjum Anand to the *Daily Mail*, 2007**

Name: Anjum Anand

Date and place of birth: 1972 in London, but grew up in Geneva, Switzerland

Background: Anjum's businessman father relocated the family back to Britain when she was 15 so Anjum could study for her GCSEs. After school, she took a degree in European business administration.

How she started cooking: Anjum taught herself to cook in her early twenties when she was trying to lose weight. Her aim was to recreate the authentic, home-cooked food her mother used to make, but in a far healthier way. The more she cooked, the more she enjoyed it. Anjum ended up leaving her office job and going to work in restaurants in New York, Delhi and Los Angeles.

Big break: Anjum was determined to write a cookbook to share her ideas. She received over 30 rejections from publishers, but never gave up hope and *Indian Every Day: Light Healthy Indian Food* was finally published in 2003.

Popular TV shows: She started appearing regularly on UKTV's *Great Food Live* show, which led to an offer from the BBC to make her own series, *Indian Food Made Easy* (2007), and a second series in 2008.

Major achievements: Anjum has made the idea of cooking Indian food at home seem simple and achievable. She is the UK's best-known Indian cook.

Something you might not know about her: Before she turned to cookery full time, Anjum worked for a company importing flat-pack furniture from Eastern Europe.

Anjum's love of food grew from her desire to recreate healthy versions of her mother's home-cooked recipes.

Anjum Anand has a diet to thank for her success. Unhappy in her job, and more than 30kg overweight, she turned her attention to the kitchen. She took the recipes she had grown up with, and stripped them to their clearest, cleanest, lowest-fat essentials. Anjum lost the weight, and found a new career.

The next step was to learn her trade as a cook. Anjum worked in the kitchen of the influential Café Spice restaurant in New York, and for the famous Thai chef Tommy Tang at the Mondrian hotel in Los Angeles.

Anjum's ambition was not to open her own restaurant and win a Michelin star. She simply wanted to share her discoveries with the world. So when she returned to England, she wrote her first cookbook, but for a long time struggled to find a publisher. Eventually she was signed by a literary agent, who supported the project, and *Indian Every Day* was finally published in 2003.

Anjum started to appear on TV cookery shows, and was a regular guest on UKTV's *Great Food Live* from 2003–2007. She was then offered her own show. The BBC2 series *Indian Food Made Easy* was a big hit, and the accompanying recipe book sold more than 30,000 copies and was such a massive success that it knocked *Harry Potter* off Amazon's number one spot. Her next book, *Anjum's New Indian* (2008) was another big seller, and was followed by a second series of *Indian Food Made Easy* in the same year.

Anjum worked with Birds Eye as a consultant chef to help develop their healthy range of Indian ready meals in 2005. She is a regular guest on the Good Food Channel's *Market Kitchen* and is also a regular contributor to *The Times Online* food pages. She is now branching out and plans to launch her own range of sauces free from additives and preservatives. Anjum is without a doubt Britain's most popular Indian cook.

"[Anjum's] popularity is largely due to the way she adapts traditional Indian recipes to help fit cooking good food into a hectic, modern lifestyle."

Anitha Sethi in the *Guardian*, 2008

Jamie Oliver
The kitchen campaigner

Jamie's cookbooks have taken him round the world – from Los Angeles, California to South Yorkshire!

> **"If you really like food, there's nothing like getting a job in a local restaurant or pub. What I learned in my dad's pub when I was working for my pocket money, I still use today."**
>
> **Jamie Oliver to Judith Easton in the *Guardian*, 2009**

Name: James Trevor 'Jamie' Oliver MBE

Date and place of birth: 27 May 1975 in Clavering, Essex

Background: Jamie is dyslexic, and left school at 16 with no qualifications, but he won a place at Westminster Catering College and could chop vegetables faster than his lecturers.

How he started cooking: Jamie's parents ran a pub, The Cricketers, and Jamie worked in the kitchen. From the age of 14 he was helping the head chef prepare a hundred meals in an evening.

Big break: His first job out of catering college was as a pastry chef at Antonio Carluccio's restaurant in Covent Garden, London. From there he moved to the River Café in Fulham as a sous (deputy) chef where he was spotted by the BBC and given his own TV show, *The Naked Chef*.

Popular TV shows: Jamie presented three series of *The Naked Chef* from 1999–2001. He then fronted *Jamie's Kitchen* (2002), in which he trained a group of disadvantaged youngsters to work in his new restaurant Fifteen. His next major series was *Jamie's School Dinners* (2005), which turned the issue of healthy school dinners into a political debate. More recently, he has presented *Jamie's Ministry Of Food* (2008), teaching the locals of Rotherham, South Yorkshire, how to eat more healthily. *Jamie's American Road Trip* (2009) and *Jamie Oliver's Food Revolution* (2009–10) are his latest shows.

Major achievements: *Jamie's School Dinners* changed government policy and improved the meals served in schools. After the show, the government pledged to invest £280 million.

Something you might not know about him: Jamie's three daughters are called Poppy Honey, Daisy Boo and Petal Blossom Rainbow.

The chirpy chappy with the social conscience and several million pounds in the bank, Jamie Oliver is probably the country's most important celebrity chef. His TV programmes are not only entertaining, but often try to make real changes to our relationship with food. His cookbooks are bestsellers, he publishes a monthly *Jamie Magazine*, and his chain of Italian restaurants is now opening across the Far East. Not bad for an Essex boy who was bottom of the class at school because of his dyslexia.

Jamie developed his love for cooking working in his parents' pub kitchen. He was always a hard worker and a shrewd businessman – he even rented extra lockers at school and ran his own unofficial tuckshop! At 16, he went to catering college, and from there went straight into some of London's most prestigious kitchens. His first job was with Italian restaurant owner Antonio Carluccio and from there he moved to Ruth Rogers' and the late Rose Gray's Michelin-starred River Café in Fulham, West London.

While working at the River Café, Jamie was spotted by a BBC producer and was soon the star of his own TV series *The Naked Chef*. 'Naked' was a reference to the simple, unprocessed ingredients that Jamie used in his recipes, but the headline-grabbing title, along with Jamie's cool clothes, Vespa scooter and his new way of talking – 'pukka' meaning 'brilliant' was a big favourite – all helped Jamie become an overnight TV success.

In 2000, Jamie became the face of Sainsbury's supermarket, a job worth an estimated £1 million per year, and something he is still doing to this day. Then in 2002, he gambled with his cuddly, non-threatening TV image, and created *Fifteen* – a documentary series that followed him training 15 aspiring chefs who were either school dropouts, homeless or ex-offenders. The show was a great success, and Jamie was awarded an MBE in 2003.

Jamie is committed to keeping food on the political agenda. He fronted *Jamie's School Dinners* (2005), where he campaigned for fresh, nutritious school dinners to help fight obesity in youngsters. He also presented *Jamie's Fowl Dinners* (2008), attempting to get Britons to eat more free-range and organic chickens and less battery-farmed birds. This chef is never far from the headlines.

Jamie learned the basics of cooking in the kitchen of his parents' pub.

"Fifteen enabled [Jamie] to reinvent himself as a visionary with a social conscience ... He reinvented himself again with *Jamie's Dinners*, his brilliant series on school food. This time, he took on the politicians and beat them hands down."

Simon Hatterstone, the *Guardian*, 2005

James wanted to be a professional chef for as long as he can remember.

> **"My goal was to be a head chef and I achieved that when I was 21... I'm a chef by trade. That's where I started and that's where I'll end up. "**

James Martin to the *Mirror*, 2008

Name: James Martin

Date and place of birth: 30 June 1972 in Malton, North Yorkshire

Background: James grew up on a farm in Yorkshire. His father was catering manager at the local stately home, Castle Howard, and when James was 11, he helped his dad cook for the late Queen Mother.

How he started cooking: James left school at 16 to go to catering college in Scarborough, North Yorkshire, where he was named Student of the Year three years running.

Big break: He was spotted by fellow chef Antony Worrall Thompson, who brought him to London to work in his restaurants 190 Queensgate and then dell'Ugo. James then spent time in France, working in the kitchens of several chateaux, before returning to England to open his own restaurant, the Hotel and Bistro du Vin in Winchester.

Popular TV shows: In 1996, a customer at the hotel invited James to a TV audition that led to a regular slot on *Ready Steady Cook*. James has since appeared on several shows, including *Housecall* (2001-2005), *Out Of The Frying Pan* (2003-2004), *Too Many Cooks* (2004), *Yorkshire's Finest* (2004), *The Great British Village* (2007), *James Martin's Brittany* (2008) and most recently BBC1's *Saturday Kitchen*.

Major achievements: James holds the world record for carrot chopping. He peeled and chopped 22 carrots in one minute for a *Ready Steady Cook Children in Need* special.

Something you might not know about him: James has a collection of classic cars that includes an Aston Martin DB5, a 1959 Corvette and a 1997 Jordan Formula 1 car.

James has presented the popular shows *Ready Steady Cook* and *Saturday Kitchen*.

While his school friends were out enjoying themselves, James was working around the clock. He started at 6am, and often didn't finish until 2am. Then it was back to work at 6am again. That was the routine, six days a week. James lived eight miles away from the restaurant, so he often just grabbed a few hours' sleep on a bench in the kitchen then woke up and started all over again.

Then a chance encounter with a TV producer at his own Hotel and Bistro du Vin in Winchester changed James's life forever. He was handed a business card one day during service, went along to an audition, and before he knew it, James was starting out on a TV career that's currently spanned 14 years and counting.

In the early days, James divided his time between the restaurant and his TV work. Now his time is fully devoted to TV, and he has appeared in an amazing 38 different series, including the 2005 series of BBC1's *Strictly Come Dancing*, in which he came fourth with professional dance partner Camilla Dallerup.

James Martin has been cooking for as long as he can remember. His parents claim he was making Sunday lunch for them from the age of five. James thinks he was probably six before he could manage it single-handed. At eight years old, he told his mum and dad that he would be a head chef by the time he was 21, own his own restaurant when he was 35, and drive a Ferrari by the time he was 40. And this was all because he didn't think he was intelligent enough to become a vet!

James's youthful dreams came true by the time he was just 24, thanks to a lot of hard work and dedication. He was working in professional kitchens from the age of 10, excelled at catering college, and was headhunted by Antony Worrall Thompson as soon as he qualified, to come to London to be his pastry chef.

James's most significant cooking series include *Ready Steady Cook*, *Saturday Kitchen* – which helped rejuvenate Saturday morning television – *Sweet Baby James* (2007), focusing on desserts, puddings and cakes, and *James Martin's Christmas Feasts* (2007). He's the hardest-working chef on TV!

"As a determined young chef, James never had the time to do anything but work ... He knew if he wanted to make it in the restaurant world, he'd have to work like a slave before he could really start enjoying life like he does now."

This is Hampshire magazine, 2006

Nigella Lawson
The domestic goddess

Although she is not a trained chef, Nigella's cookbooks fly off the shelves!

> **"Cooking is ... about developing an understanding of food, a sense of assurance in the kitchen, about the simple desire to make yourself something to eat ...You must please yourself to please others."**
>
> **Nigella Lawson, 2006**

Name: Nigella Lucy Lawson

Date and place of birth: 6 January 1960, in London

Background: Nigella moved schools nine times between the ages of 9 and 18. Nevertheless, she was skilled academically and went on to study medieval and modern languages at Oxford. After graduating, she worked at the *Spectator*, first as a book reviewer, and then as their restaurant critic. She went on to become deputy literary editor of *The Sunday Times* in 1986.

How she started cooking: Nigella is not a trained chef, and does not see herself as an expert in her field. However, her mother was an enthusiastic cook, and Nigella is very comfortable and confident in the kitchen. She came up with the idea of her first cookbook, *How To Eat* (1998), when she saw a dinner party host in tears over a messed-up dessert.

Big break: *How To Eat* sold 300,000 copies in the UK, and was followed by *How to be a Domestic Goddess* in 2000. The book sold 180,000 copies and won her Author of the Year at the 2001 British Book Awards. The success of both books led to her first TV series, *Nigella Bites* (Channel 4) in 2000.

Popular TV shows: *Nigella Bites* (2000-2001), *Nigella* (2005), *Nigella Feasts* (2006), *Nigella's Christmas Kitchen* (2006 and 2008), *Nigella Express* (2007).

Major achievements: Nigella won a World Food Media award and a Guild of Food Writers award for the first series of *Nigella Bites*.

Something you might not know about her: Nigella is the daughter of Baron Lawson of Blaby, and is entitled to be called 'The Honourable Nigella Lawson'.

Nigella Lawson has never won a Michelin star, never run her own restaurant, never even studied cooking. What she has instead, is an infectious enthusiasm for food – both making it and eating it – that has helped her become one of the country's most popular food writers and broadcasters.

The daughter of a Conservative politician (who later became Chancellor of the Exchequer), Nigella started her career as a journalist. Her first job was book reviewer for the *Spectator* and then, when they asked her to expand her role, their restaurant critic. She chose food writing almost by accident. She remembered a description of champagne in one of her favourite books as 'tasting like apples peeled with a steel knife' and decided it would be interesting to write about food herself.

After a spell as *The Sunday Times'* deputy literary editor, she became a freelance writer, producing a food column for *Vogue* and working with *Gourmet* and *Bon Appetit* magazines in the United States. Her first cookbook, *How To Eat* (1998), was a great success and was called 'the most valuable culinary guide published this decade'. The follow-up, *How to be a Domestic Goddess* (2000), beat bigger-name writers like J.K. Rowling to an Author of the Year prize.

Nigella's real success, however, came when she took her enthusiasm, charm and considerable talent in the kitchen onto the television. *Nigella Bites*, filmed in her family kitchen in West London, ran for two series on Channel 4 in 2000 and 2001, capturing nearly two million viewers, and winning several broadcasting awards. The series also broadcast in the USA, and the book of *Nigella Bites* became America's second bestselling cookery book of Christmas 2002.

The follow-up series *Nigella Feasts* broadcast in the US in autumn 2006, and made her £2.5 million when it was bought by ten other countries around the world. The same year, she moved to the BBC to present *Nigella's Christmas Kitchen*, and more recently *Nigella Express*. Her audience are such loyal followers that sales of goose fat increased by 65 per cent, and Riesling wine by 30 per cent when Nigella included them in her recipes. For her fans, Nigella is quite simply a domestic goddess.

Nigella's TV series are broadcast in the USA and around the world. She is a global cookery star.

"Cooking is fashionable but eating less so. [Nigella] loves and encourages both and serves it up with a classy garnish of joie de vivre."

In the *Telegraph*, 2007

Heston Blumenthal
The wizard in the kitchen

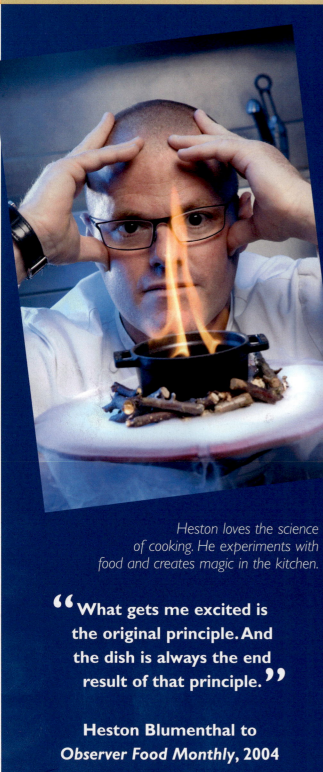

Heston loves the science of cooking. He experiments with food and creates magic in the kitchen.

> ❝ **What gets me excited is the original principle. And the dish is always the end result of that principle.** ❞
>
> **Heston Blumenthal to**
> ***Observer Food Monthly*, 2004**

Name: Heston Marc Blumenthal OBE

Date and place of birth: 27 May 1966 in High Wycombe, Buckinghamshire

Background: Heston attended the John Hampden Grammar School in High Wycombe, and Latymer Upper School in London.

How he started cooking: Heston's love of gastronomy started on a family holiday to Provence, when the family ate at a famous two Michelin-starred local restaurant. Heston was hooked. He left school at 16 and did a week's work experience in Raymond Blanc's kitchen at Le Manoir Aux Quat' Saisons in Oxfordshire. He then worked at a selection of jobs from trainee architect to photocopier salesman, and spent all his spare time learning to cook.

Big break: In 1995, Heston saved enough money to buy a 450-year-old pub called The Fat Duck in Bray, Berkshire and started to cook professionally. The Fat Duck started life as a classic French restaurant, but Heston's fascination with the science of cooking and the origins of flavour led to amazing and original dishes like bacon and egg ice-cream and snail porridge.

Popular TV shows: He has presented *In Search Of Perfection* (2006) and *Further Adventures In Search Of Perfection* (2007) for the BBC, *Big Chef Takes On Little Chef* (2009) and *Heston's Feasts* (2009-10) for Channel 4.

Major achievements: The Fat Duck achieved the fastest three stars in British Michelin history. It went from one to three stars in just five years.

Something you might not know about him: Heston was awarded an OBE in 2006 for his contribution to British Gastronomy.

Bacon and egg ice cream and snail porridge are two of Heston's best known and most original recipes.

Heston Blumenthal looks like a nightclub security guard, but cooks like a wizard. His culinary inventions like sardines-on-toast sorbet, basil blancmange and beetroot jelly are not just headline-catching, they taste good too and have made him and his restaurant famous. The Fat Duck in Bray, Berkshire has won three Michelin stars, received a 10 out of 10 score in the 2010 Good Food Guide, and been voted number 1 in the San Pellegrino World's 50 Best Restaurants.

Unlike the majority of his peers, Heston did not serve a cooking apprenticeship in one of the great kitchens. He was not a protégé of an inspirational chef like Marco Pierre White or Raymond Blanc. Instead, Heston learned his cooking from books. He was always fascinated by the science of cooking - what is happening on a molecular level when meat browns, soufflé rises and fat melts - and in 1986 he discovered *On Food And Cooking* by American writer Harold McGee.

Heston used these experiments, along with his interest in vacuum (sous-vide) cooking – whereby a joint of meat is cooked for up to 24 hours at a very low temperature to retain the fat content, and keep the meat tender – to develop a whole new way of approaching food and cooking.

His endless enthusiasm and inquisitiveness led to two successful BBC series *In Search Of Perfection* (2006) and *Further Adventures In Search Of Perfection* (2007), where Heston tried to recreate and improve classic British dinners, including bangers and mash, spaghetti Bolognese and chicken tikka masala.

Next came the challenge of updating the Little Chef motorway restaurants for the Channel 4 show *Big Chef Takes On Little Chef* (2009). Most recently, he has made *Heston's Feasts*, where he recreated and updated Roman, Medieval and Tudor recipes, cooking dormouse, baking blackbirds in a pie, and serving cow brain custard.

Heston also owns The Hinds Head in Bray, which serves more traditional pub food, and despite all his work commitments, says he is always home for roast dinner on Sundays with his wife Suzanna, and their three teenage children. How he cooks it is anyone's guess!

"Blumenthal may be using kit that would look more at home in the laboratory than the kitchen. He may be combining flavours in a way that will surprise and disorientate. But if it's not good eating, he's not interested, however futuristic it might be."

Jay Rayner in the *Observer*, 2006

Hugh Fearnley-Whittingstall
The countryside cook

Hugh and his family moved out of London to River Cottage in Dorset in 1997 to start a new life.

"At no point did I ever make a career plan, but I was always keen to write and interested in food, so it was kind of pretty obvious."

Hugh Fearnley-Whittingstall to the *Guardian*, 2006

Name: Hugh Christopher Edmund Fearnley-Whittingstall

Date and place of birth: 14 January 1965 in Hampstead, London

Background: Hugh's parents moved the family out to Gloucestershire when he was six. He went to the exclusive private school Eton, and then to St Peter's College, Oxford, to study philosophy and psychology.

How he started cooking: After graduating from university, Hugh spent time in Africa, working in wildlife conservation. On his return to the UK, he got a job as a trainee chef at the River Café in Fulham. He had no formal training, but was offered the position on the strength of a tart he cooked for his interview! Hugh didn't adapt well to the demands of the River Café kitchen and left after six months.

Big break: Hugh spent time as a freelance journalist in London, before moving his family to Netherbury in Dorset. They lived in a former gamekeeper's lodge called River Cottage, and Hugh's attempts to become self-sufficient and live off the land growing his own vegetables and rearing his own animals became a popular series of TV programmes and best-selling books.

Popular TV shows: *Escape to River Cottage* (1999), *Return to River Cottage* (2000), *River Cottage Forever* (2002), *Beyond River Cottage* (2004), *River Cottage Spring* (2008), *River Cottage: Winter's On The Way* (2009).

Major achievements: Hugh is an active campaigner against intensive farming, and fronts the Chicken Out! campaign against battery farming.

Something you might not know about him: Hugh was in the year above Prime Minister David Cameron at Eton.

A campaigner for animal rights, Hugh is strongly opposed to intensive farming.

FREEDOM?
vote for Resolution 17!

attempts to 'live off the land'. He digs up his flower garden to make a vegetable plot, hunts pigeons, stalks roe deer, raises and slaughters pigs, sets up beehives to collect honey and much more besides.

The format of the shows, mixing a fly-on-the-wall documentary with Hugh's own back-to-basics, locally sourced, often organic recipes, made each series a real success for Channel 4. The accompanying cookbooks even earned Hugh a rumoured £2 million advance (the amount paid by the publisher to the author before the book is published). He is the author of the best-selling books, *The River Cottage Cookbook* (2001), *The River Cottage Family Cookbook* (2005) aimed at parents to use with their children, and *River Cottage Every Day* (2009) among others.

Hugh has become increasingly involved in the movement to raise awareness of intensive farming methods. He has appeared on several series of Gordon Ramsay's *The F-Word*, giving advice on the rearing of turkeys, pigs and lambs. More recently, he has campaigned to encourage people to eat free-range chicken. He even became a shareholder of Tesco, so he could try and force the supermarket to only sell free-range and organic birds.

Hugh Fearnley-Whittingstall has made a living out of living off the land. Like the much-loved 1970s comedy series *The Good Life*, Hugh and his family quit the 'rat race' in London, moved to the country and made plans to be self-sufficient. Hugh's habit of picking up roadkill and eating berries he found in hedgerows has even earned him the nickname Hugh Fearlessly-Eatsitall.

In 1997 Hugh and his family moved out of London and settled in Dorset, in a former gamekeeper's cottage in the grounds of Slape Manor in Netherbury. River Cottage, as it was known, had previously been the family's weekend getaway, but now they were here for good! The first four series of the *River Cottage* (1998-2004) followed Hugh's

Hugh, his wife Marie and their two sons and adopted daughter now live on a 37-acre farm near Colyton in Devon. The River Cottage adventure continues!

"The only TV chef I think delivers anything with integrity is Hugh Fearnley-Whittingstall. He is romantic ... he is intelligent, he shows the provenance of food."

Marco Pierre White in the *Radio Times*, 2007

Sophie Dahl

The new cook on the block

Sophie's grandfather, children's author Roald Dahl, taught her that food should be fun and exciting.

" The food I love to both cook and eat is totally simple. I like straightforward, honest food ... geared towards mood. Cooking should be an adventure. **"**

Sophie Dahl on *The Delicious Miss Dahl*, 2010

Name: Sophie Holloway, now Dahl

Date and place of birth: 15 September 1977 in London

Background: Sophie is the daughter of actor Julian Holloway and writer Tessa Dahl. Her grandfather on her mother's side was world-famous children's author Roald Dahl, who named the heroine in BFG after Sophie. Her parents divorced when she was young, and Sophie attended ten different schools and lived in 17 different homes from London to New York to India, as she travelled the world with her mother.

How she started cooking: Sophie has never trained professionally but she has always cooked. She has the ability to use food to emphasise happiness, remember long-lost memories, and to bring loved ones together. She writes a weekly food column for the *Saturday Times*, and is a columnist for *Waitrose Food Illustrated* magazine.

Big break: Sophie had written two fictional books, *The Man With The Dancing Eyes* (2003) and *Playing With The Grown-Ups* (2008), before her first cookbook, *Miss Dahl's Voluptuous Delights*, was published in 2009.

Popular TV shows: Sophie's debut cookery show was *The Delicious Miss Dahl* (2010), produced by Jamie Oliver's Fresh One production company. The show, first broadcast on BBC2 in March 2010, featured a mix of recipes from her cookbook, along with some 'personal food memories'.

Major achievements: Sophie has successfully changed direction from modelling to writing and presenting, and looks to be the next celebrity chef who everyone will be talking about.

Something you might not know about her: Sophie is married to the jazz singer and pianist Jamie Cullum.

Sophie Dahl has been a supermodel, a children's book heroine, and now perhaps is Britain's next big celebrity chef. Her six-part TV series *The Delicious Miss Dahl* (2010) ran on BBC2 and won her an army of new fans. The show featured recipes like beetroot soup, omelette Arnold Bennett and peanut butter fudge from her cookbook *Miss Dahl's Voluptuous Delights* (2009).

Sophie writes and presents with warmth and enthusiasm. Like Nigella Lawson, who she is regularly compared to, Sophie has no formal cooking training, but she wins over viewers with her charm and sense of humour, as much as for her obvious love of food.

Sophie's first job, at 18 years old, was as a model. She was discovered by a stylist for *Vogue* magazine, and introduced to the owner of Storm, Kate Moss's long-term model agency. Before she knew it, the 6 foot tall, size 14 Sophie was working for huge household names from Yves Saint-Laurent and Versace to Alexander McQueen and The Gap. She lived in New York, and became – not by her own choice – a spokesperson for 'normal' sized women everywhere. When most fashion models were constantly dieting, Sophie ate takeaways for two, and loved eating in restaurants.

Gradually, though, Sophie started to leave modelling behind, and indulge the two biggest loves of her life – writing and food. Her interest in cooking began in her childhood. Grandfather Roald Dahl would make her jellies mixed with crunchy hundreds and thousands, and ended every meal with chocolate. Her grandmother Gee-Gee insisted on three meals a day, fresh vegetables and no snacks.

Sophie's real skill is not in cooking, but in making the food she cooks and writes about a much-loved part of our lives. The taste of fudge, the smell of a Spanish omelette, can unlock treasured memories and transport us to certain key points in our lives. If there was a Michelin star for likeability, Sophie would be a worthy winner.

Sophie's favourite recipes are usually simple, indulgent and enjoyable. Her love of food is infectious.

"*Miss Dahl's Voluptuous Delights* is part recipe collection, part food memoir that makes you feel good about food... Beautifully shot and well-written... [it's] a thoughtful book by an enthusiastic food fan."

The Observer, 2009

Other Celebrity Chefs

Rick Stein

Christopher Richard 'Rick' Stein (born 4 January 1947) is a chef, restaurant owner and TV presenter based in Padstow, Cornwall. He grew up in the Cotswolds, and studied English at Oxford University. However, the family spent their summers in Padstow, and Rick moved to the town with his wife Jill after graduating. Although the pair are no longer married, they still run three restaurants together, as well as a hotel and a seafood cookery school in the town. The most famous are The Seafood Restaurant, opened in 1974, and his fish and chip shop. Rick has such a positive effect on the local economy that the town is nicknamed 'Padstein'.

Rick made his first TV appearance in 1985, with a guest slot on fellow chef Keith Floyd's *Floyd on Fish* for BBC1. Ten years later, the show's producer was looking for a new idea for a series and got back in touch. The result was *Taste Of The Sea* (1995), which won a Glenfiddich Award for TV Programme of the Year. Rick has since appeared in a number of award-winning series, including *Fruits Of The Sea* (1997), *Rick Stein's Seafood Lover's Guide* (2000) and *Rick Stein's Food Heroes* (2002). Rick Stein's successful cookbooks include, *Rick Stein's French Odyssey* (2005), *Rick Stein's Mediterranean Escapes* (2007), *Rick Stein Coast to Coast* (2008) and *Rick Stein's Far Eastern Odyssey* (2009).

Nigel Slater

Nigel Slater is a cook and multi-award winning food writer turned TV presenter. Born in 1958 in Wolverhampton, he moved to London at 18 and found a job in the kitchens of the Savoy hotel. For several years he moved around the country, from Yorkshire to Bristol to Cornwall, cooking, washing up and wine waiting. One of his regular customers was starting the magazine *Homes And Gardens*, and asked Nigel to check some recipes. He told her they didn't work, so she suggested he write his own.

Nigel was food writer at *Marie Claire* magazine for five years, and has written a column for the *Observer* for the last 17 years. His books include *Real Food* (2000), *The 30-Minute Cook* (2006), and the autobiography *Toast: The Story Of A Boy's Hunger* (2004), for which he won Glenfiddich Food Book of the Year, British Biography of the Year, and a WH Smith's People Choice Award. Most recently he has presented the TV series *A Taste Of My Life* (2006) and *Simple Suppers* (2009) on BBC1.

Jean-Christophe Novelli

Michelin-starred chef and TV personality, Jean-Christophe Novelli was born 22 February 1961 in Arras, France. Jean-Christophe left school at 14 to work in a local bakery, and at 20 became personal chef to the wealthy Rothschild family. He travelled the world for two years before settling in England, and becoming head chef at Keith Floyd's Malster's Arms restaurant in Totnes, Devon. From there, he moved to Le Provence in Lymington, Hampshire where he won a Michelin star, and then became head chef at London's Four Seasons Hotel, where he won a second star.

With the help of friend Marco Pierre White, Jean-Christophe opened his first restaurant, Maison Novelli, in Clerkenwell, London in 1986. He has twice been voted Chef of the Year, and the AA Chefs' Chef. Jean-Christophe made his first TV appearance on Channel 4's sports reality show, *The Games*. He then became one of two team leaders (along with Gary Rhodes) in the 2005 series of *Hell's Kitchen* (ITV1), teaching members of the public – rather than celebrities – how to cook. In 2006 he appeared on *The X-Factor: Battle Of The Stars*.

Gary Rhodes

One of Britain's best known celebrity chefs, Gary Rhodes was born 22 April 1960 in London. Gary went to catering college straight from school, and got his first job at the Amsterdam Hilton hotel. He later moved back to the UK, becoming sous chef at the Reform Club on Pall Mall in London, before earning his first Head Chef position at the Castle Hotel, Taunton in Somerset. He retained the hotel's Michelin star at just 26 years of age. In 1990 Gary moved back to London to become Head Chef at the Greenhouse where he won a second Michelin star in 1996. In 2005, Gary's successful London restaurant, Rhodes Twenty Four, won its first Michelin star. In 2008, another of Gary's restaurants, Rhodes W1, won a Michelin star bringing his current total to 6!

Gary is probably best known for his TV appearances. He has fronted shows such as *MasterChef* (2000-2001), *Hell's Kitchen* (2005) with Jean-Christophe Novelli, and several of his own series including *Rhodes Around Britain* (1996), *Rhodes Across India* (2008) and *Rhodes Across The Caribbean* (2009). Gary also swapped his chef's whites for dancing shoes to appear in the sixth series of BBC1's *Strictly Come Dancing* (2008). However, his dancing wasn't quite as good as his cooking – he only lasted until week three!

Antony Worrall Thompson

Henry Antony Cardew Worrall Thompson (born 1 May 1951 in Stratford upon Avon) is a well-known celebrity chef and TV presenter. After leaving school, he studied hotel management at Westminster College. In 1978 Antony moved to London, becoming sous chef at Brinkley's Restaurant on the Fulham Road. He became Head Chef there one year later, before taking a year's break in France to study regional cuisine. Antony opened his first restaurant, Menage A Trois, in Knightsbridge in 1981. It was famous for serving only starters and desserts!

Antony has been on our TV screens for nearly 20 years. He made his first appearance on BBC2's *Food And Drink* in the early 1990s, before joining *Ready Steady Cook* from 1994. In 2003 he appeared in the second series of ITV1's *I'm A Celebrity... Get Me Out Of Here*, and took over as host of BBC's *Saturday Kitchen* when he left the jungle. In 2006 he moved to ITV to present *Saturday Cooks!*, and more recently *Daily Cooks Challenge* (2009).

Antony is interested in promoting healthy eating. His cookbooks include, *The Essential Diabetes Cookbook* (2010) and *Antony Makes It Easy* (2010).

Thomasina Miers

Born in 1976 in Cheltenham, Gloucestershire, Thomasina Miers was the winner of the BBC's *MasterChef* in 2005. Thomasina visited Mexico at the age of 18 and became such a fan of the country and its food that she moved there. She opened a cocktail bar in Mexico City, and spent time travelling around the country and learning from great local chefs. She returned to London to make a living as a freelance food writer for *Waitrose Food Illustrated* magazine, the *Financial Times* and the *Saturday Times*.

After winning *MasterChef*, Thomasina presented two series of cookery programmes for Channel 4 with co-presenter Guy Grieve - *Wild Gourmets* (2007) and *A Cook's Tour of Spain* (2008). She has recently opened the Mexican street food cantina, Wahaca, which won the *Observer Food Monthly's* 'best cheap eats' award, and has now opened three branches in London. Her first Mexican cookbook, *Mexican Food Made Simple*, published in March 2010. Thomasina was recently described by the Mexican Ambassador to London as 'Mexico's greatest ambassador.'

Index

21st Century Lives

Contents of books in the series: